All These Colors
By

InfiniteTeal

A light hearted story about two artists and the meaning of colors on emotions.

WHITE

White- cold and unfriendly, bland and sterile, pure and innocent.

I sat in class, staring blankly on the wall as everyone started drawing their sketches for their project. I just wanted to get straight to the painting, I wanted to get the colors down on canvas, but I had to sketch what I wanted to draw first. I stared down at my blank paper finally, knowing that I might just have to wait till I get home since I need more than this environmental conversation. I should just wait.

I put my pen down and sighed quietly in the silence. I should work hard but I don't know why I've lost motivation; maybe this sort of thing isn't for me. I should just try something else.

But I love all the paint, and the colors. That's what gets me to do what I need to. I want to paint everywhere.

The bell rang and everyone shuffled up, causing a debris of noise that killed the silence. I got up too, putting my pens in my bag as I took my books. As I backed away from my seat, I bumped into someone, causing them to drop their stuff.

"I am so sorry, I didn't mean to-" I hurried to state my excuse but Eli was already reaching for his stuff quietly.

"Don't worry." he said as he got his papers together.

Eli is a prodigy, someone who takes art to the next level. I look up to him, everyone does, Mr. Phillips loves him because of what he can do. But Eli is sort of a bit weird. I notice he doesn't talk much to people, he stays on his own a lot. He doesn't hang out with anyone, he doesn't even notice us. And sometimes, he can be a bit squirmish around people. He's Haphephobic. He has a fear of being touched by people. Its something I picked up on not too long ago. It isn't extreme, but I know he has other problems as well. ADHD, OCD, all the works.

He isn't terribly afraid.

I bumped into him and he didn't start screaming. At least he knows its an accident. And he got his papers organized neatly.

When he stood up straight again, he tried his best to smile, but I saw he didn't get there. He isn't a people person, I know that too. I don't feel bad for him, he is a nice person though. Just slightly crazy. I stared at his pink lips that were curving slightly on his pale face. He had dimples the size of craters which literally were about to dominate his cheeks. I haven't seen that before.

"I didn't mean to...ah, well... I'm sorry about bumping into you." I said quickly, hoping he knew how sorry I was for something like this.

"Its fine." he said as he turned away from me. Well, he tried at least. That's a start. I watched him walk away, his slick black curls moving as he moved.

Eli Vander is someone no one can get to.

The only reason I know about his problems is because my mom works at a mental hospital. She knows all the phobias and extreme disorders. I learned a lot over there, and sometimes, I see them in Eli as well. It makes me wonder if he should be admitted there, but he isn't crazy, just a little strange. But he draw like no other, he can paint like no one else, he can do anything with a pencil, pen, or paint brush.

His price for being so talented is his problems.

I ran my hand through my hair as I sighed to myself again. I should be getting home before it gets too crowded in the halls to leave. I took my stuff and walked out of the class room with the last people who were leaving. The day had gone by pretty slowly until my little accident happened. I should stop being such a klutz towards people more and things won't be so terrible.

I walked home on my own. This town is sort of small, not a lot of people reside here. Its always quiet, and no one does much. Its boring too, buts that's what its like. The trees are the same, the cars are the same, the houses are the same. White, blue, and yellow, all the colors that are on houses, or on things, or just everywhere. I know people who live in each house, on each street. Its friendlier I guess. I would hate to be in the city. As I walked, I greeted the people that I knew, and the people I didn't. Its like this everyday.

And on the other side of the street, Eli was walking the other way, going a different way home.

I heard he doesn't have a family, that he lives by himself, that he makes money by himself. Its just himself. I never asked him so I wouldn't know what was real or fake, but I want to know though. I want to know how he gets by, why he's the way he is, why he can do art better than anyone I've ever seen. But that's his business. He doesn't talk, so I can't expect much from him.

I barely even know him.

I walked inside my house quietly, hearing mom talking on the phone since no one replied to her questions. Dad was probably still working. He's a psychologist, so he studies human behavior and functions. He tells me things too, and I think its interesting because I can apply it all. I dropped my bag as I thought some more about all this. I wanted to ask mom some questions, but I know she's busy so I should hold it.

Instead, I took my sketch book out of my bag, and found a few different pens that I could use for shading. I went up to my room, intending to draw for the rest of the day without any disruptions.

But after a while, I found myself sketching Eli's face lightly. If I could paint this, I would. I would use turquoise for his eyes, and add in a soft green around the edges. Black for his hair that curled thickly, strands loosely falling around his bright eyes and close to his nose. A dark grey color for his eye brows and thick eye lashes. A light shade of brown, almost pale brown for his skin, and a slightly darker shade to shadow in his dimples. And then pink for his lips. I didn't think I would be able to sketch him that fast, but I ached to paint him. But I can't do that. I tore the paper off and tossed it on the floor, focusing on the project instead.

It didn't take me long to get distracted, but after a while, I ignored it and moved on.

The next morning, I was hesitant to go to school. I was hesitant of going to my last class. Art. I wanted to continued drawing him but I didn't want to be a creeper. I held in my sudden urges, but maybe I could at least be his friend. I don't have a reason for doing this other than I want and I really do want to. Being completely alone can cause insanity.

So at the end of the day, I walked into my next class, sort of eager to talk to him. So eager that I got ahead of myself. I had more intended now.

"Hi…um-" I sort of got nervous when he looked up at me. He was still quiet, waiting on me to finish since I clearly was not done. But him looking at me was the one thing that made me stop. I need to collect myself before I look like an idiot. "Would you mind if I sat with you today?" I asked.

He didn't answer.

Then he moved his stuff to free open the seat right next to him. Hopefully I didn't seem to desperate to sit here, but maybe I could talk to him. I could already tell his boundaries even though he didn't make it specific. As the bell rang, I sat next to him quietly, putting my bag on the table, making sure it didn't touch his stuff. No physical contact, no pushy questions, don't make him feel uncomfortable.

"So why would you want to sit next to me?" he asked quietly as Mr. Phillips began talking to the class.

"I wanted to talk to you." I admitted quietly. Isn't that how friendships start? I stared at my hands, twirling an ink pen around as I completely disregarded Mr. Phillips words.

"I'm not that interesting." he whispered.

"I don't believe that." I said and looked at him. He just might be one of the nicest people on this world, I just want to know if that's true or not. His blue eyes scanned my face for a second then they moved somewhere else, away from me.

"Eli, Jamie, since you're already sitting together, you two can be partners." Mr. Phillips said as he moved on around the class. I hadn't known he was doing that. I didn't even know we were getting a minor assignment today.

"I didn't predict that either." I said quickly to Eli.

"Its okay, I'll take care of the whole thing." he said.

"Don't do that, I can help you." I said. I know he's some sort of art god, but it would be terrible of me to make him do all the work because of it. I didn't plan this happening so I have to put my two cents in anyway.

"Are you sure?" he asked. I wonder if he's asking about my well being in general. The way he asked it said that I might not be prepared to work with him mentally. But it should be fun, at least, that's what I thought it to be.

"I can't let you do everything yourself." I said and meant it. I wouldn't ever make him do this on his own. Even if its a minor project. "And I don't completely suck at this." I added to be funny. And I was. He smiled and laughed.

"A lot of people know that." he said as he pulled out his sketch book, flipping to a blank page.

But the page before it caught my attention first. I was careful not to touch him but I wanted to see the portrait before it. I flipped the page back slowly, finding a sketch of a face almost as accurate as a picture.

My face.

I stared in shock. Not because he drew my face which means he thought of me, but because it was the most amazing sketch someone has ever done of my face. How did he remember everything so perfectly? I could be staring at a mirror basically. He drew my hair all messy like it was yesterday. My eyes were big and I bet would be colored blue. He drew my nose right too with the freckles around it and cheeks. He drew me smiling too, and it made my cheeks look bigger, and basically my face looked brighter because of that. And the pens he used for this didn't make me want to paint it at all, I loved the vague colors he used. I stared longer than I should have since it gave away my amazement.

"This is amazing, Eli." I said quietly.

"At least you don't find it creepy that I somehow manage to draw your face in detail." he said and I heard a sarcastic tone to it. I don't find it creepy because I did the same thing. I reached in my messy bag and took my sketch book, flipping to the last page with something drawn on it.

I showed him how I had drawn his face last night.

"You planned on coloring it." he said.

How'd he know?

"I did, but I just thought that it would be too much. Its already creepy enough." I said and laughed lightly. He was quiet for a moment, thinking as he pulled his lips in a hard line.

"Do you...want to come over to my place later...to work on the assignment?" he asked. I wonder how big a step this was for him, because it doesn't seem like he asks people that for sure.

"Sure." I answered because I was interested. I already know we won't be working on that project anyway.

But it would be nice to get to know Eli more and go to his place.

ORANGE

Orange- energetic and excitement, blatant and vulgar, warmth and attentive.

We walked to his place. Eli isn't as quiet as I thought he was. He isn't shy, his personality needs to be pushed out. He is very bright. And the way he talks about things with such imagery makes me forget reality for just a little while. I liked hearing him talk and get excited about things, it was nice. He had a vision for a good bit of the things he talked about, and it was a passionate vision. No wonder he is talented. I was amazed to know how he thinks and feels.

I was aware of his slight problems though. It wasn't hard to figure out. His focus was hard to control, he even told me that. His fear of people wasn't bad, but he described it to not be a fear, just a precaution. He really doesn't like other people touching him but he said he's working on that.

What he wants is to be more interactive with others.

At least he's trying and succeeding. He isn't anti social at all.

I told him about me, what I knew about me at least. There wasn't much though. I'm pretty normal in the sense of boring. The only thing he thought was amusing was the fact that my mom and dad work with mental problems. And he has mental problems. But they aren't extreme as other people I have met.

He has a regular loft place, something usually college students would live in. It was big and a little empty but I have to remember he's the only one who lives here. I saw the small kitchen with the white refrigerator and silver appliances around. It doesn't seem like he uses them a lot. And when I walked further inside, I saw a messy bed, some papers on the floor, some paint bottles and water bottles, some clothes and other things on the wooden floor.

I had my back towards another wall. When I turned around, I almost dropped my stuff just as quickly as I dropped my jaw. It wasn't some plain old wall, it was a painted wall. There was a painting of big flowers on the wall. They were orange and dark red and bright yellow. But the center was mostly orange. I noticed other paintings on the corners and sides, and almost as if it was under the flowers. He paints over his paintings sometimes, he must use the wall all the time I stared at the wall, and then my eyes went to the floor.

"Sorry for the mess, I didn't expect you to say yes to me." Eli said as he walked by me.

"No its fine- how do you do that?" I pointed to the wall because that was my main focus at the moment. I haven't seen people do this to a wall in their own place before. And he is constantly painting over it.

"Well," he started, glancing towards the wall as he thought of answer to my question, "I just sort of paint whenever I'm in the mood for it I guess." he said as he walked over to it. "This was two days ago." he added, sighing.

He always does this?

"Its amazing." I said quickly.

"I'm probably going to paint over it again." he said as he looked down at the paint colors on the floor.

"You don't have canvases?" I asked.

"I do, but I use those for other things." he said as he picked up a paint brush that was in some cyan paint. He has a whole set of blue.

He flung blue paint on to the wall, not caring about messing with the perfectly painted flowers. The orange color made me feel sort of anxious but after seeing the blue, I was conflicted. I wasn't sure if I should be calm or not. The colors were contrasting each other but warm and cool colors aren't mixed plainly like that.

I walked next to him, picking up another paint brush. I dipped it in the cyan paint and walked up closer to the wall; I drew a big line over the orange flowers, crossing over them without any tension in my wrist. I liked it.

I didn't think I would actually enjoy painting on someone else's wall but there was so much room. I drew a thick line over the flowers and for some reason, it just felt exhilarating. It was like I had all this space to do what I wanted.

Elijah must get this feeling a lot.

"I can't believe you live here." I said in some sort of shock. It finally reached me. I turned around towards him and found him twirling his paint brush as he began smiling at me.

"Its a bit simplistic." he said.

But he took this wall and made it into something that wasn't simple. It was beautiful. Does he know that?

I noticed some different bottles on the floor close to under his bed. They weren't tucked that far under. I moved around the paint tubes and cans and walked across the loft to look at them. I was a bit suspicious of them. And when I picked one up, I was right with my suspicion. Alcohol.

"You drink?" I asked as I read the bottle. Its vodka.

"I learned its hereditary." he said.

I looked over to him. He said it's hereditary. "Your parents were alcoholics?" I asked.

"They both were. My dad practically killed himself by drinking." He sighed as he looked away. "And my mom just follows wherever the alcohol is." He rubbed the back of his neck as he turned away from me completely.

Being an alcoholic can be hereditary. Should I be surprised that its already started for him? He might have that dependency on alcohol now, or even years ago. I would have never thought he was a drinker, it doesn't seem like he's a heavy drinker, but I just don't know. I'm not sure. I put the bottle back down on the floor lightly as I noticed more of them. I can't comment on his habits. I barely know him and its not my place to say anything about it.

"I'm sorry." were the only words I managed to get out of my mouth.

"I should have known it was coming. But its fine. I try not to drink so much. And if I really feel like it, well..." he turned to the wall. He paints to get rid of the frustration. He does art to get rid of the frustration. I admire that

He tries not to fall victim to his problems. Instead of moping about it, he tries to make it work.

"How long does it take you to do all this?" I asked.

"If I'm really focused, not that long." he said. I walked back over next to him and picked up the paint brush I had before in my hand. I wanted to draw all over it. I just wanted to put my feelings on this wall.

I never do this.

But I want to.

"Go ahead." he said, already feeling my anticipation for all this. When he said those words I got closer to the wall, putting my blue stained paint brush on it. He did the same too.

And we painted on his wall.

For so long, I was just attracted to the wall, wanting to do this for a while. And as it began to get dark, the blue turned out to look much better with the mixed orange. We left spots for the orange and red and yellow to peak out of but the wall was mostly blue where the warm colors dominated. I contained myself as best as I could, but after a while, I started to let my emotions out. I was calmer now because of the blue instead of anxious. It made me feel better than I was before.

I will always want to do this.

We sat on the floor together, staring up at the wall as it got darker and darker inside. It was getting late but I wanted to stare at the wall. I had gotten paint on my arms and my clothes, but that's the one thing I enjoy about painting: getting dirty. Eli had paint on himself too, and I thought blue complimented him but that's because of his eyes, his bright blue eyes.

"For once, what I did doesn't look so bland." I admitted.

"Its better to add emotion in. That's what art is." he said as he drew the paint brush on his arm, drawing streaks of blue on his skin.

"It feels better." I said, watching the wall then glancing at him. He seemed more at peace. This is why he does it, right? I found it interesting because its him. Because its all him.

"That's when you know you did it right." he said quietly as he put his paint brush down. "We didn't even work on the assignment." he said. I covered my face as I curled up. I forgot all about that.

But I knew that would happen.

"Don't worry about it, I can do something tonight." he said as he got up.

"I can't make you-"

"You're not." he said. I noticed he held his hand out for me to take and he wasn't hesitant about it either. Is this a good idea?.I took his hand slowly and he helped me up. "I'm still working on it." he said when I noticed he was slightly shaking. I took my hand from him so I wouldn't scare him even more.

"I don't want to make you uncomfortable." I said.

"You don't." he said and tried to smile. He's working on it. "I'll walk you home." he said. He really is trying.

I thought about being home, then I wondered how my parents are taking it right now. I should have been home a while ago, I didn't even call to say that I would be late for dinner. That's a slip up on my part. But hopefully I won't get yelled at.

I took Eli's offer to be walked home.

If I could be with him longer, I would. It was fun being with him. I wonder if he knows that at all. I think he's entertaining, and fun, and he's really passionate about art. I thought it was cool. I want to do this more often but I can't be picky about it. I don't want to push my luck and ward him off about it, Eli is a really great person and I don't want to mess up what we have right now.

"Thank you for walking me home." I said as we walked up my front steps together.

"Thank you for wasting time with me." he said, laughing lightly. In the dim light, I could see his smile, and the way his eyes shined when he was happy. I looked up at him with amazement and I didn't even realize I was doing it.

"It was my pleasure of course." I said and looked down, almost feeling myself blush. I didn't know why I was doing that but I was.

"I'll see you tomorrow, Jamie." he said and began to turn the other way. I caught a glimpse of his perfect smile as he walked down the steps. I held back my wave when he couldn't see me anymore.

I wanted to do this again.

I walked inside quietly, only to find yelling the second I stepped in. I wasn't surprised at all by this, in fact, it happens. I don't really go out much and when I do, I come home to yelling. And its directed towards me so I shouldn't be shocked by it in the slightest.

"Jamie, where were you?" Mom came to greet me harshly. I notice that she was in her white uniform, as if she just got back from work. Of course she did.

"I was with a friend." I said to her as I put my stuff down.

"For that long?" she asked.

"We were working on something together." I said.

"I can see that." she looked me up. Its not like I can hide the paint that stained my skin and clothes. I didn't mind it though, I liked the paint on my skin. I always liked it. But mom doesn't, she finds it disturbing. Very. I watched her look me up as if she was sort of intrigued and scared at the same time.

"I'm sorry mom, I-"

"No, I'm sure it was something you enjoyed doing, since you couldn't even let us know you were going to be gone for so long." she said as she crossed her arms, turning away to walk on. I can't really fight with my mother, its not something I will win. I picked up my bag and dragged it along as I went upstairs.

This paint wasn't going to come off for a while. I didn't mind though.

BLUE

Blue- calm and serenity, sad and aloofness, tranquility and security.

I struggled to get all the paint off my skin, but after a while, I stopped and got dressed for school. I know mom will hate it because she sure did hate seeing me stained with paint last night. She and dad gave me all kinds of psychological reasons for my obsession with painting but in about this point in my life, I'm just going to disregard those comments.

My parents know I want to study art, but basically in a psychological way unfortunately since it just runs in our blood. The way art makes me people feel, the way colors make people feel, its all different but the same. I just want to know why, and how. I would love to do that.

I walked down stairs, playing with the sleeves to my plaid shirt so they would cover up to my wrists at least. There was still a lot of paint on me and I had no time to get rid of it. I got into the kitchen, finding that my parents were about ready to leave for work.

"Jamie-"

"I'm sorry, it was hard to get off. I didn't know it would be that tough." I said quickly before they could say anything.

"I was just going to tell you that I might be coming home late tonight." Mom said. "Something you should have done yesterday." she added in because she is still mad about that.

"I'm sorry. I was working on something." I said and looked away as I rubbed the back of my neck.

"Are you lying, Jamie?" she asked quickly.

"No." I answered.

"Yes he is." Dad said.

I tried but they don't believe me and that's what's wrong with having parents with psychological knowledge. They think a lot of things, cautious of other things. I won't get by with just the truth.

"I was working on an art project." I said.

"That part may be true." Dad said.

"Okay, I'm going to be late for school if I don't get going." I said and took my bag. Mom was going to say that was a lie too but I walked out before she had anything else to add.

I got outside and took a breath of fresh air. The sky was a bright blue color today, and there were no clouds. I felt lighter and wanted to paint the sky but it wouldn't take me long to do that. I continued to stare for a little bit, then I realized I would really being late if I just stand here and look dumb. I walked on, ruffling my hair as looked away.

I should worry about my other classes more but I didn't in a sense that I didn't have to. I guess art is more important, I like that class the most but now I like it even more than before. I guess its because I know someone who likes it even more than I possibly can in my life time.

Eli is just a reason why I'm seeing this as even more important.

I couldn't even wait to sit in Art but I had to wait throughout the day. I kept doodling in class when I was supposed to pay attention but I was bored and wanted to do something fun instead. All this isn't for me, but I have to suck it up anyway and try to deal with it as best as I can. Its only a couple hours to get to Art, I can deal with it.

When the time finally came, I walked in slowly but eagerly. I saw people turning in work and it just occurred to me that Eli basically took care of our little project. Its not fair for me to make him do that. Plus Mr. Phillips will know that I had absolutely no effort in this in the first place because I can barely do what Eli can in one night. Hopefully he doesn't catch on to it, or maybe he won't care much. If there's a next time, I'll know my part in this.

I sat in the seat that I sat in yesterday, hoping Eli won't mind that at all. Maybe if I look innocent enough, he won't be mad I guess. Or a bit nervous. I was calm about it, I sat down without regret and I let the world go round while I did that. He walked back to his seat, a smile almost on his lips, but it didn't quite get there unfortunately.

"What did Mr. Phillips say?" I asked quietly.

"Well I told him it was your idea and I just drew it up. He said that it shouldn't happen like that again." he said.

"Which means there's a next time." I said.

"Which means it might happen again." he said. Eli didn't care about that did he? Its just a minor project, he has better things to create. Like the project that's fifty percent of our grade. I have to get started on that.

"I can't let you draw everything for me." I said as I turned in my seat to look at him. He glanced my way, his blue eyes scanning my face. And then he looked away from me.

"It doesn't really matter." he said.

"Yeah it does, Eli. I have to put in whatever crap I can." I said as I put my bag on the table, noticing the class quiet down as Mr. Phillips was about to tell us about what we're going to do today.

"Okay, so I know he's going to make us do another partnered assignment. How about you do it this time." he suggested. Nice. I laughed to myself, playing with my sleeves as I pondered on this.

"I can do that then." I said because it will be a great thing. Although, he's going to have to settle for a ninety because Mr. Phillips always finds something to be subjective about.

"Which means you'll be coming with me." he added in quietly.

"Eli-"

"Or we could go to your place." he said. I stared at him for a second, knowing that I was giving away that we were talking. "Its been a while since I've been in a real home." he added in quietly.

"I would love to have you over, and you know, paint my room, but..." I looked down. I have a concern about this whole thing. "Its just that my parents can be judgers." I admitted.

"And so is the rest of the world." he said.

"No I mean, out loud judgers. They will rip you apart verbally, and analyze you medically without putting a finger on you. This is why I don't bring friends home." I explained quickly. My parents have being giving psychological issues to people just by watching their behaviors and I can't take it when they do that.

"That's interesting." he said and meant it.

"Its abuse." I corrected.

I remember the first time I told them I was going to take art seriously and they literally gave me reasons why this was happening, why I was quitting sports, why I was hanging with less and less friends, why I gave up on some things. And what makes me terribly mad is that they're right. I wanted to do it because I had an obsession for it. I wanted to get better at it, to study it, to know everything about it. That's what.

"Then my place it is. Though I really should have cleaned up this time." he said and looked down, thinking. It wasn't such a mess. My room is pretty terrible I guess. And its just me, I'm not worth it anyway.

"I don't mind."

"Its not kind."

"I don't care." I said and proved that very well. I really don't care what his loft looks like or what kind of mess there is. I just don't care. "My room is pretty dirty." I said quietly, playing with the strings on my bag.

"I should sneak in some time." he said. I held in my laughter as best as I could. But that would be funny for him to just sneak into my room through the window. How entertaining would that be?

But it would be cool.

We could just draw and talk about things. That's what I would like.

But I said nothing to it since I had nothing to say about it. I chose not to say anything anyway. I held in a sigh too, but I kept smiling about it. Eli is pretty cool, I wonder if he knows that. He isn't so bad, I never even thought he was in the first place. But he's better than I thought he was.

We walked together after school let out. Today went by smoothly, no problems, no stress. It was just calm and serene more than anything else. I wonder if he feels the same thing that I do. How can anyone not though. I can't be the only to feel how nice it is outside. No one can come out here and be mad. Just breathing outside made me feel calm. Nothing could make me feel any different.

Eli wasn't as hesitant as he was the first day when I bumped into him but I was careful to still not touch him. I know it might be a bit much for him still but its fine.

The paint on the wall was still there, mostly blue with orange dots. The cool color was engulfing the warm ones. I thought it was amazing how we could do that, I wonder what we could paint next. I put my bag down on the counter as I noticed a bunch of papers on the floor.

"I think I should have food here." Eli said and wandered off. If he doesn't, that's fine with me. But I was preoccupied with looking at something. I walked over to the mess of papers by his bed side. All of them had faces on them, all of them portraits.

All of them me.

I picked them up, a bit amazed that he drew so many and knew all my faces. I didn't think I had faces like that but he was somehow able to capture them all. I stared at them, and I thought it was a reflection of my physical and emotional being. How does Eli do that? Its like he captured my emotion as well. I looked at the last one. It was me looking down but smiling, that movement I do when I find something entertaining but don't want to say anything about it. How could he make me look like this? I liked this better than my actual appearance.

I held in a sigh.

He draws me when I'm not even around to see him do it.

I think that's talent. I just wonder how he can remember me like that. Is it a bad thing to want to keep these? I planned on it but he has them for a reason I guess. Why take them? I should probably work on my skills, that's if I have any in the first place.

"Why do you just draw me?" I asked when I saw him again, near the fridge.

"I'm sorry, I know its creepy." he said.

"Well, you draw me when I'm not around, which is pretty amazing for what, the second day? But you know, I could always just sit down and you could draw that way." I said, looking at all the sketches again. All these perfect sketches.

"Wouldn't it be the same from memory?" he asked.

"I don't know how that's true for you." I said, sort of shocked. I found it amazing that he could do that. He can put in so much emotion in this and not feel anything. Is that how he does it?

"Okay, how about this." he said as he came over to me, picking up a sketch book on the floor and a black ink pen. "You can start on that partnered assignment and I can try to do this right." he said. I looked down, laughing to myself, then I realized I'm doing the exact same thing he captured before.

"You'll probably be finished faster than me." I said as I sat down on the floor, taking a sheet of blank paper from his book and finding another pen. I don't know what I should be doing for this, and I don't want to let Eli down.

"Then I'll be slow about it." he said and sat down in front of me.

"I don't even know what I should be drawing." I admitting, staring at the blank paper. I completely zoned out while Mr. Phillips was giving instructions. No, I was talking to Eli the whole time.

"Well, you're supposed to draw something peaceful, something that makes you feel calm." he said. I thought about it. This has to do with emotions, so I really have to try. And I can't be a beginner with what I pick, it should be complex, right? I thought hard.

And then I noticed that Eli was already drawing me. The heat rose around my neck and up to my face since I knew he was watching me. I could hear the pen on paper, and basically feel his eyes on me. I had to think of something, I couldn't just sit here.

The first thing that came to mind, I drew.

I thought of birds flying in the blue, clear sky, a bunch of black birds all together in their families, just flying up on the paper. It would be plain but I liked it. What I looked forward to was coloring it mostly. I had it all planned out.

I could use two different pens for this. Color light and dark, add in some shading.

It made me want to do this more.

I guess I got excited but I focused more on drawing, letting my pen touch the paper, ink it with black against white. I liked it.

And Eli drew me as I did our assignment. I don't know what it was, but I was comfortable with him glancing at me to see my face, my features, my emotions. It should be better than just guessing, but its for me as well. Sitting in front of him didn't make me feel weird at all, and that's what was interesting. I wanted to see how he was drawing me, but it would only make me blush harder. Its a good thing he isn't going to color me because he would notice my flush face. I already feel it. I colored in the small birds as I heard his pen hitting his paper. I couldn't get anxious, the only thing I felt was peace.

I kept telling myself I didn't mind, and I truly didn't.

Eli makes me feel calmer. And somehow, I can do whatever I wanted freely around him, except touch him of course, I can't do that. But anything else is fine right.

"Are you done yet?" I asked, losing my focus. Its been a while and I know he can do a pretty good sketch after a while. He still drew though, and as he did that, he smiled lightly. He finally did it. I wanted to get it down on paper but I couldn't right now. I just stared at his face as he continued to smile. His dimples popped out more as he got into it.

"Don't tell me you're the impatient type." he said.

"I'm more curious actually." I said. He still smiled and I watched. I couldn't stop looking at his face, or his blue eyes, or his black curly hair. I couldn't stop looking at all of him. I tilted my head to the side as I didn't move my eyes. This is odd but I knew it well.

"Your thoughtful face is my favorite right now." he said and handed me the sketch book. I was amazed with what he drew. It will always be like looking in a mirror, so much that its unreal. He was able to make me start thinking again, just by looking at this. Somehow, it looked like my eyes could shine brightly if he colored it dark green and darkened my eyelashes.

"This is so unreal. How do you put so much emotion in this with just a couple glances?" I asked.

"Art is emotion. And emotion is art." he said quietly.

"This is amazing." I said, staring at it. This is something I can learn from him. Art is emotion. I should really learn that more since the last four years haven't been helping me one bit. "I should really focus on this kind of stuff more, it would be better if I did." I said.

"Or," he started as he got up. "You could worry about keeping that thoughtful face of yours." he said, holding his hand out to me to help me up. I took it without hesitating this time, and let him lift me up. He's touching me longer, he wasn't even letting go of my hand. He was slightly shaking but he didn't stop.

"Are you sure that-"

"Its the only way I can get over it, right?" he smiled a bit as he looked down. I know he can try without needing extra help. Well, he's the only person I know trying without getting extra help.

"Its a good thing you're trying at least." I said as I looked down at our hands. He wasn't moving away from me at all. And I really liked that honestly.

"I might as well. Sometimes, I just get consumed in it. Other times, I work with it. Today must be a good day." he shrugged. He amazes me. He's going to be fine. His disorders aren't over powering to the point of no return at least.

"Lets make everyday a good day, okay." I said and smiled up at him. He started to smile, his eyes sparkling. Does Eli know he could look like this?

I should really get this in ink.

PINK

Pink- love and romance, affection and infatuation, happiness and passion.

A few days of being around Eli is all I need to feel the overwhelming power of what its like to really know what art is. He is serious, but he loves it. It keeps him sane, it keeps him from doing something he shouldn't.

He tells me things.

Sometimes he gets terrible thoughts, or craves to drink, and sometimes, he can't win. I just want him to know that I'm there for him. He probably knows that already I bet. I look out for him, and make sure he doesn't drink. I usually find him drawing on the wall, throwing paint around and smiling.

Sometimes, he's smiling and I smell alcohol on him.

Sometimes, he's just quiet.

Eli wasn't kidding with me when he said he barely has any control. But he isn't hurting himself, and that's a good thing. I want to make sure he's okay because he's my friend and I care for him more than he could know. I want to be there for him. Its not like he stops me, he lets me in his life which is unusual; he has no secrets, nothing I should be scared about. Just nothing. And its a good thing, but it makes me worry.

I was doodling in my room.

Well not doodling. Over three days, I drew a better portrait of Eli, and I liked it so much that I started coloring it. I had all my pens over my bed and I picked the blues first. His eyes are something I like the most, he holds all his emotion there, and that's where he sees through me. He can figure out my deepest feelings and bring it to life buy inking it on paper. Its those eyes that keep me near him.

I heard shuffling by my window but I didn't stir or get scared over it.

Eli has been sneaking into my room like he promised a while ago. He is certainly living up to his words. I'll let him come through the front door when I know my parents won't be judgmental and terribly embarrassing. Eli doesn't deserve to be analyzed, no one does, but that's what my parents do. And its terrible since they do it out loud without any respect or regards to anyone's feelings.

I glanced up at Eli as he made his way to my bed after he shut my window. His black leather jacket made him look much badder, as if he could fight anyone and win against them. I stared at his dark choice of clothing, and then to his black curly hair that was messy around his face.

"You're still working on that?" he asked as he sat down next to me.

"Well, its not perfect yet, so I have to perfect it." I said as I colored the edges of his eyes with a darker blue, making it appear to shine more with the colors in the middle.

"There's a project that's fifty percent of your grade due soon." he said.

"I'll start some other day." I blew it off. I usually do it the week of the due date. Something tells me I might need more time. But I liked coloring in Eli's eyes. I think they're gorgeous like this. I never thought that I could draw his eyes so beautifully, its almost as if they were real. I glanced up at him again to see his eyes.

And I noticed he was watching me.

"Are you going to draw another portrait of me again?" I asked as I looked down at my paper.

"I have enough of those lying around." he said, laughing to himself. I know he does have a lot around, I see them. I take some sometimes, but I let him have the ones he likes. "But I came to try something." he said quietly. I looked at him because he sounded unsettling, like he wasn't sure. And when he didn't look at me, I put my things on the bed so he could have my full attention.

"What do you want to try?" I asked when he kept his silence going.

"Well um... I..." he looked away, still thinking about it. He shouldn't be scared around me if that's what it is. "I don't know. Maybe I shouldn't." he said quickly.

"No, go ahead. I won't mind whatever you want to try." I said, being considerate since he was thinking seriously about this.

He bit his lip as he began to be indecisive. I won't pressure him to try whatever he wants to. It must be something difficult if he can't decide whether to do it or not. But when and if he does, I'll be here for whatever it is because I'm his friend and that's what friends are for. He doesn't have to think so hard, I don't want him to hurt himself over it.

But I noticed him getting closer to me after he took a breath. I didn't stop him because after a second, I knew what he was going to do. I closed my eyes, keeping my thought process down. If he wants to do this, then I will not stop him. I can't. But I don't want to at the same time.

He kissed me lightly, his lips soft as they pressed against mine. That was the only contact we had, he didn't touch me anywhere else, I didn't try to either. But him kissing me was enough for me.

It was different, but of course it would be, I'm not surprised. But I liked the feeling of his lips on mine, I liked the way he kissed me slowly as if I was something delicate. I wanted to do indulge in it so much.

My fingers twitched on the bed. I wanted so badly to touch him, to run my hands through his hair, to caress his cheeks, to make him stay near me. But it won't happen the way I think it will. I can wait though. But my fingers kept twitching anyway. I would do anything to feel his face.

I got more ahead of myself just because of my excitement for Eli kissing me. He wasn't shocked or alarmed, he let me kiss him back.

I didn't think that we would be doing this at all. I didn't think he liked me that way, I didn't think I liked him that way either. I was nervous about this because its the closest I've been with him. I wasn't nervous seconds ago but now I was going to blow up.

If I make one wrong move, I might screw it up.

But I didn't think that before my body took over.

I moved my arms, just about to wrap them around his neck, but he knew what I was going to do and pulled away from me quickly. I shouldn't have done that, I really shouldn't have. I knew he would be uncomfortable with that, but I couldn't help it. He had gotten up and moved away from, moving to the middle of my room as he rubbed the back his neck. It seemed like he regretted kissing me. I don't.

"I'm sorry, I shouldn't have..." he trailed off and I knew this was just bad.

"Please don't be sorry." I said, almost desperate. I didn't think he would be apologizing out of all the things he could be doing. "I don't mind. I really don't." I said as I got up, hoping I can just make him feel better.

"Don't say that." he said quietly as he looked at me. I guess he was betting on me to be repulsed or disgusted.

But I don't mind that he touched me or kissed me. I don't care.

"Eli-"

"I like you." he said. "I like you a lot and I just wanted to know if it was worth it." he said.

It is.

Well I want it to be.

I took the couple steps between us hesitantly, hoping that he wouldn't be scared of me coming closer to him. I didn't want to push my luck and make things worse for him, but I wanted to show him that I do like him and I don't care about it. He shouldn't be worried about me. His blue watched me come closer to him, and as I moved my hands, I watched him take a slight breath, but he didn't move. I touched his face lightly, pulling closer to him until I felt my lips on his.

He let me kiss him this way but I wasn't going to make it last long. I just like the feeling of his lips on mine, I like the sweetness and the softness of him. I would love to enjoy it as long as I could, but I don't want to put pressure on it. After a few seconds of kissing him, I let go and pulled away slightly. I kept my eyes closed since I could feel him so close near me.

"Goodnight, Jamie." he said quietly, his warm breath hitting my skin.

I didn't want him to leave but I didn't try to stop him from going. I guess he might just need a little bit of time. I watched him separate from me, going to my window and leaving. I held in my voice so I wouldn't blurt anything stupid.

I sighed to myself and ran my hand through my hair.

I just hope this doesn't change anything about us. I hope nothing goes wrong.

The next day, Eli didn't show up at school. It made me wonder if it was because of last night. In fact, I didn't have to wonder, I already knew. I decided to go see him, if he would let me at least. After school, I walked to his place. It was bright outside, so I thought it would be a nice day. But Eli wasn't here so it wasn't that nice, it was sort of boring. He has to have a good reason for skipping school, hopefully other than not being able to see my face. I don't think its that bad.

I like Eli. And he wouldn't have kissed me if he didn't feel the same about me in the slightest.

He didn't answer to my knocks, but what I noticed was that the door was unlocked. If its like that, then there's a problem. I opened the door and walked inside the quiet loft. He has to be here. I closed the door and walked further inside, looking around until I saw him sitting at his bed side, holding a bottle in his hands. He looked tired, and sort of sad.

The wall was pink, a light color pink and white flowers. It was beautiful but it didn't match his mood.

"Why are you drinking?" I asked. He sighed and ran his hand through his hair.

He caved.

"Eli." I said when he didn't say anything.

"I got tired." he was lying. I dropped my bag to the floor and walked over to him slowly; I took the bottle from his hands lightly and he didn't fight me.

"You should have called me." I said.

"I didn't want to bother you." He lied again. He doesn't want me to know or see him get anxious. This is the part I'm not used to but I have to be.

"You don't have to think that." I said and put the bottle on the ground. He kept his eyes away from me, not even wanting to try. "I always tell you I don't care, I'll always be here." I said.

"I know... I just..." he stopped himself and that's what made me a bit sad. He doesn't have to worry.

But I can't be the one to pressure him.

I turned around, and looked at the wall instead. All the pink and white. They're softer colors, lighter colors. Sweeter and delicate. I wonder why he would pick those colors, I wonder why he painted flowers again. I walked closer and looked at all the paint cans on the floor. The red paint can was opened. It was a deeper red, almost like blood, but a bit brighter. I liked the color. It was very aggressive.

"I started the major project." I said and turned around. "I'm doing a collage." I said.

"Drawing it?"

"Only way." I said and kicked my feet around lightly. My project shouldn't take long to finish, but that's if I don't sleep from now until its due. Which is possible that I won't.

"That's a good idea." he said.

"You're done with yours aren't you?" I asked, being a bit bland.

"I haven't even decided on what I want to do." he said, looking down at his fingers. I know it will be the greatest thing anyone could put their eyes on. "But there should be time." he said. I walked over to him, and took hold of his hands. He didn't shake or wrench away; he let me pull him up.

"You should take a shower and get rid of that awful alcohol smell so we can go outside." I said, wrinkling my nose as I smoothed out the wrinkles on his shirt.

"Jamie-"

"Please?" I asked. He didn't deny me after that. I want to walk with Eli and go places since we weren't together at school today.

"Okay." he said quietly.

While he was gone, I got rid of whatever alcohol I could find, dumping it down the sink. Something might happen if he drinks too much, I'm just lucky that I got to him before. I know that I can handle that problem of his, and I know he will let me.

BROWN

Brown- strength and reliability, warmth and comfort, isolation and security.

The wall changes every couple of days, just like always. I had gotten paint on my clothes and things, but I didn't mind it much. I stared at the wall, amazed with what we were able to accomplish together.

A tree, a big rooted tree. Its roots dig into the dirt, grabbing and hanging on to its life, to what it needs. It doesn't want to let go because it will only mean death for it. It is blooming with leaves and flowers, but there was more emphasis on the shades of brown; the bark, the ground, the dirt, the roots, branches, everything. This tree needed to stay grounded, it needed to be with the earth, to become one. It won't be able to live without it, so it hangs on tightly.

Eli liked the tree.

And it reminded me of him.

Eli desperately holds on a lot of times. He makes sure to keep himself alive when he knows he can't take it anymore. He has a different case of depression, its something unusual; I would have never thought of him to be depressed, not in the slightest. He didn't have to tell me this either, I figured it out. Maybe he isn't depressed, it just might be his mood since he doesn't know, but I think it might be depression.

Is it because of his parents?

His alcoholism?

What makes him so sad? How can I help? I glanced at him occasionally, watching his blue eyes look over the wall as he sat there in silence.

I got up, not wanting to disturb him since he looked like he was in serious thought. Instead, I walked to couple sheets of paper that were spread out by his bed side, the ones I had ignored when I came a couple hours ago. I already knew what they were, but I just wanted to see them. Eli draws a lot of portraits about me, and I can barely finish one in a couple days. But these were so nice, I wanted to keep them.

Eli is very talented. And he has literally put a dent in my life.

I like and care for him. I would hate it if something were to happen to him and I couldn't stop it. I glanced over at him, seeing him run his hand through his hair and sigh as he got up. This tree will be gone in a matter of days and he will do something better than what was there before. He will never be satisfied with what is on that wall.

"Its going to rain later." I said as he walked over to me.

"I should walk you home." he said and I knew he would too. I bet he just wants to be in the rain, but I do too. It would look nice.

"We'll get sick." I said, but he was going to get an umbrella anyway. I sighed, almost laughing as he played with the black umbrella in his hand. It matched his messy black hair that he didn't care to fix. All the curls were there though.

"This should be fine right?" He asked.

"Its pretty bad out there." I said. He shrugged again, smiling lightly as he pulled me on.

What was funny was that we didn't even use the umbrella.

We walked in the rain as if we couldn't feel it, even though we could. And we didn't care. Eli was happy and I liked seeing him like that, I like seeing him smile and laugh more. I realized how rare it really is to see him smile because most the time, he barely does it; he's either drunk, stagnant, or thinking to hard in his creative mind. So in this rain, I watched him smile and laugh while I did it with him. It would only last for so long.

When we got to my house, that's when we finally decided to start rushing. It was cold and we were drenched in water as if the sky had turned over into the sea and dumped it all on us. All I desperately wanted was to get out the rain and into some dry clothes. I pulled Eli on with me. My parents weren't home and I wouldn't care that much even if they were, I think its okay for him to meet them, or for them to meet him. I don't care.

"Gosh, its cold." My teeth chattered on their own as I stumbled into my room. I'm starting to wonder again why we just walked slowly instead of running as quickly as we could to get out of there. I went into my closet and pulled a ton of clothes out, throwing them on my bed.

"We probably shouldn't do that again." Eli said behind me.

"We could have used the umbrella." I said, hoping that he knew that we could. When I turned around to look at him, I saw that he had his back to me, taking his shirt off and shaking his damp hair. I tilted my head to the side as I stared at his back.

I have never thought of someone's back as being attractive before.

I didn't think Eli was as muscular as he was showing me right now. As he took off his shirt, I could see every muscle of his arms and back and it made me go blank. I don't just stop thinking like that but I had to pause because because I didn't know what I was doing. I couldn't even do anything at the moment.

When he turned around to pick one of my shirts up to put on, I looked away quickly, feeling my face heat up as I began taking off my clothes. I haven't felt this way before so its new. I hope he doesn't see how I'm blushing, it will only make everything so embarrassing.

"Your clothes are a bit small." he said.

"I'm sorry, I'm not really that big." I said sheepishly as I got over being flustered as quickly as I possibly could. But he probably did notice which made me somehow weary about it.

"I know." he said as he came over to me. I shrugged my shirt on as I noticed how he was trying to tower over me. He might be taller but not by much. I'm close enough to him by height.

I could smell him still even though I thought the rain would have washed it away. And for once, he didn't smell of alcohol. I would love to step closer to him, but I didn't. I just fixed the wrinkles out of his shirt like I always do. He's been letting me touch him more and more which means he's more comfortable with me. I like that.

"I guess we're staying here all day. And I don't have a wall to paint." I sighed.

"We can take a break from all the art right now." he said quietly and I knew what he meant, well sort of. I wasn't surprised when he stayed this close to me, I even wanted him to be closer but that's when I made the first move.

"How subtle." I murmured; I heard his low laugh as he returned my actions, kissing me softly as I felt his curving lips on mine. I'm sure I'm going to think about this, then want to draw it as desperately as I want to kiss him.

This is my mind now, I want to get it all done.

If I could get all my feelings down as best as Eli could, I wouldn't be longing so much. But that wasn't all of it.

I tasted the rain water on his lips just with the sweetness. As his hands moved to my sides, my body moved with them, feeling the tingling sensation I get when he touches me. I kissed him back, wanting him more and more, wanting to feel him more. I was more attached than I usually am, but kissing him is like pure bliss. I wanted it.

He pressed me against the wall as I wrapped my arms around his neck lightly, pulling him down to me so I could kiss him more, harder. The way he kissed me, the way I kissed him back, this isn't something we should be doing but we were doing it. I tightened my arms when I thought about how much closer I wanted to be to him.

I didn't like how he pulled away from me, but then I felt his lips at my neck and I didn't stop him. My fingers twisted in his hair as he kissed my skin hungrily, almost making me grab him more.

How is he making me feel this way? All this heat was driving me insane, it wouldn't stop. My body burned under his, and it was only going to get hotter. I gasped for air, trying my hardest to not let him devour me, but it was happening and I wanted him.

I was shocked to know he had a wilder side, a more aggressive side. I liked it just as his more gentler side. I liked all of him.

Before I knew it though, I could hear my parents down stairs. They're home. Eli knew when to stop, I didn't want him to. I wanted him to keep going and make me feel hotter, but we can't anymore. His breath got on my neck as we processed what just happened. This wasn't normal, but I know I wanted to keep this going anyway. But my parents are home and we can't risk anything.

I fixed my shirt that was rising up on my hips and looked away. My face was probably incredibly red right now but I wasn't surprised by that at all. Eli kissed me with much more passion than he has before and I enjoyed something like that to the fullest, that is, until my parents got here.

"They're here." I sighed silently, running my hand through my wet hair as I avoided eye contact with Eli. He knows that I was doing it too, I make it obvious unfortunately.

"I can go through the window." He said as if it really was an option.

"No no, its raining, and you don't need to get wet again." I said, completely disregarding his suggestion to leave that way. There is literally one option left which is go downstairs. "Do you just want to say hi because they're going to come up here to check up on me anyway." I said.

"Would that be a good idea?" he asked.

"Just try to avoid physical contact, and if it doesn't work, just don't let them know about it." I said quickly.

One thing Eli can be have a hard time with is not giving away his reactions to certain things that make him very uncomfortable, like being touched. Sometimes, it works out, other times, it doesn't. He's gotten better with controlling his slight abnormalities but I don't want him doing that just because he's afraid of my parents analyzing him. They will do that anyway. I want to hope that Eli has that sort of thing under control so I don't have to do much.

We walked down stairs quietly; mom was telling dad a story about a new patient that was admitted into the hospital where she works. She said that she was the craziest of all the people she has met in all her ten years of working there. My parents live off the minds of the strange and corrupt. I wanted to just turn around and go back to my room silently but I took a breath and held out anyway.

"Jamie, its nice to know you acknowledge our existence." Mom said. I bet she was still mad at me because I never tell her that I'm going to be with Eli. "And you finally brought home a friend." she said, a tone to her voice.

"Yeah, um. This is Eli." I said to her feeling her eyes burn through me deeply.

"I hear a lot about you." Mom said to him. I wanted to cover my face but I didn't. "You're the artist." she said as if to give a little more about what she knows. Of course.

"I am." Eli said.

"Well its nice to meet you." Dad took over and I knew it wasn't going to be any better than what it was with mom. But dad held his hand out for Eli to shake and I was just glad that Eli didn't hesitate. He did shake his hand.

I stared into dad's eyes to see if he would be doing something he shouldn't. But through his glasses, it didn't look like anything, he was just being polite for once. I was grateful but I give it ten more seconds.

"Why is your hair wet, Jamie?" Mom asked.

"I was outside in the rain." I said to her plainly. Just having that come out of my mouth made her very upset with me and I wanted to be sorry but mom will find something else wrong and fix it.

"You're always doing something." Mom said and I know she was going to add on to that. Sometimes, when we have guests, she censors her statements but most of the time, it never happens.

Instead of saying anymore and making things worse, I took Eli's hand and pulled him on with me, heading back upstairs before anything terrible happened. I was lucky enough to have them not say anything about Eli but it truly won't last long. I quickly got him up to my room because I just couldn't take being down there, its unbearable first of all.

"Well they're my parents, lets never ever do that again." I said and ran my hand through my hair.

"They don't-"

"They are." I said quickly. He thinks they might not be that had when they are. They just get into people's minds and crush them mentally which makes me very upset for the most part.

"They seem like nice people." he said as he went around my room, finding all my colored pens and taking some paper.

"Eli-"

"I want to draw something." he said and sat on my bed. It could take a little while so I might as well do something productive. I took a piece of white paper and a black pen as I got into bed, leaning on the pillows.

I know what I wanted to do with this time.

I pictured earlier when he took off his shirt, when I saw his back and all his muscles. It made me go blank but that was perfect since that's what I need to draw this out. I outlined a sketch first, drawing exactly what I could see in my head.

And when that was perfect, I drew in the details.

Every single detail I could remember.

All the lines, and the curves, and veins. The tension of when he took it off, and when he grabbed the other shirt. It was as close to seeing his real body. I drew his hair that was damp against the back of his neck, dripping with water. His pants had hung low on his waist, showing more detail than I thought I could get. I drew that too and made sure to get it right.

I didn't feel bad about getting this down on paper.

I didn't feel embarrassed either. It was going to happen.

Eli turned to me after a while and showed me what he worked on. It was me talking to my mom downstairs. How did he get that? I stared at my face and then her face. Its like we had unspoken words, something we wanted to say. And in my eyes, I seemed desperate. But I don't know for what. She was like that too, but she was tougher than I was, her expression hardened where mine was plain.

"You love your parents." He said.

"I never said I didn't." I said.

"I know." he said as he watched me become consumed in this one piece of paper. Right now, it revealed everything I couldn't figure out. It made me wonder about everything.

As I stared at this, Eli took the paper that was on my lap. I had no justified reason for drawing that, and I wasn't going to find one at a time like this but he can stare all he wants.

"I think you exaggerated." he said. That is something I actually cannot do. I laughed a little bit as I put the paper down.

"I don't exaggerate," I said truthfully. I drew what I saw and that's the truth. He started to smile a bit as he thought. And I bet he was thinking that I truly wasn't capable of drawing something like this. Either that or he's trying to think if its really true. It is though.

"You over did it." he said.

"Then you clearly don't know your own body." I said and took the paper back. I just might have to add it to my collection of subtle Eli works. I don't have nearly as much as he does of me but its enough.

We just like drawing things and each other, although I will never be as good as Eli. He id completely out of my league when it comes to what we do. But I can always try. I like drawing him, I like getting his features down, his emotions, everything about it.

He kept smiling at me; this was the face that I enjoyed so much, the face that I wanted to draw a hundred times over. His smile, his dimples, his white teeth, his damp curly hair. His body. He doesn't understand how much I longed to do this.

After a while of laughing and commenting on features, we stopped and started kissing. And I liked doing that, and he did too. It was nice to have him close to me like this. I like him more than he could possibly know but I wonder what I mean to him. I think it might be the same, hopefully.

RED

Red- deep and dramatic, anger and aggression, intensity and strong.

Eli wasn't in school today. Unfortunately, I couldn't go immediately from school to go see him because my mom wanted me to accompany her at work. That wasn't something I was interested in at the moment but she was making me go anyway and I can't say no.

Eli swore to me that he wasn't drunk but I have to see it to believe it, and I really did want to make sure he wasn't drinking. I want to make sure that he's alright and not doing something he isn't supposed to. I know I don't know how his mind fully works but I know that once he can't take all the thoughts, he tries to shut them out completely. And when one way doesn't work, he uses the other as if it will. I thought I got rid of all the alcohol but I had a gut feeling that I didn't. I just want to look out for Eli but I can't when my mom is here lecturing me about my future as a psychologist.

The second I was able to leave, I did. And I didn't stay home either, I wanted to go see Eli because I hadn't seen him all day, not once. I saw him yesterday and he was fine but when he doesn't show up to school, I know he might just be sitting around and thinking too hard when he doesn't have to. I almost started running over to his place because I was that terrified of something happening to him.

When I walked into his loft, I just noticed the unbearable silence. Was he even here? I dropped my bag on the floor and looked around.

"Eli?" I asked as I looked around hesitantly.

"Yeah?"

He was in front of the wall, that was now holding a different simple picture. It was the one I drew for the minor class assignment a few weeks ago. Black and white. The small birds just flying off into the sky. Eli made it bigger and better. I wonder how he feels right now, I wonder what's in his head.

And I wondered why his hands were dripping red paint onto the floor covered with paper.

"Why are your hands soaked in red paint?" I asked.

"I was going to use red but I got lazy." he said as he continued to stare at the wall. His hands were covered in the deep red paint, almost like the color of blood. Every second, a drop of the dark red paint fell to the floor.

"Its a nice color." I said as I went and stood next to him. I didn't think it was typical of him to be paint free but he was; the only thing painted on his body was his hands. I stared down at them, liking the dark color.

"Its intense." he said, moving his hands. And then I took one hand in mine. Paint dripped all the way down my arm to my elbow, and dropped to the floor, one at a time. The red liquid dripped from his arm as well. When I took his other hand in mine, more paint spilled and it was just getting on me.

I started to laugh lightly because I like getting paint on me, if anything, its a nice feeling. He liked it too, he wouldn't be smiling if he didn't.

He came closer to me, and soon he kissed me. For a second, I forgot about the paint, and I put my hands on his face. He started laughing lightly as he put his hands on me too, putting more red paint on my neck and face. We couldn't stop laughing and kissing and getting each other colored in red paint. I drew on his cheek, feeling the paint smear on our skin as he touched me. His hands reached my waist now, pulling on my shirt lightly.

That's when it got deeper than I thought it would.

He didn't let go of me, and I didn't want to. I kept my body close to his as I kissed him with much more passion than he thought I could give. He tasted sweet on my lips, not like alcohol. I had the urge to move my tongue over his lip, and I was hesitant, but when I tasted inside his mouth, I melted since he returned the favor. Eli doesn't really do that, but he finally did and I took up on this.

We kissed desperately, every second making us want to keep doing this. His hands had tightened at my waist, pulling my body closer until I couldn't feel any space between us. I started to pull on his hair when his tongue reached further in my mouth. I desperately wanted him to keep going. His lips weren't gentle on mine anymore, he was more aggressive than he has been.

I liked it.

We started moving around, getting to his bed without breaking what was going on. I still kissed him just as fiercely as I felt him pull me down with him. His body was over mine, making me want him much more. His fingers tugged at my shirt still, as if he wanted it off me. But I wasn't sure. I still started to try and get it off me and soon he began to help me.

He was taking my clothes off and I wanted him to. My fingers gained a mind of their own and moved in his shirt, feeling his soft skin of his toned body. I haven't been able to do something like that, and I didn't think I would be able to. But I took it upon myself anyway just to feel as much of him as I could. I wanted to feel all of him.

His hands traced my body, making me tense slightly as his fingers reached to my pants. He stopped kissing me when he got there; I felt his breath on my skin just then as he paused. I was the one gasping but he was the one thinking cause I wasn't. I couldn't.

"I want you." I whispered quietly.

"Are you sure?" he asked. All he wanted was my approval in the first place. I would never think that something like this would be a mistake, just because I really did like him a lot, more than he knows.

"I'm sure." I said, looking into his blue eyes that scanned my face. Red paint marked his skin, but I felt it on mine too. I think that's what drove us here but I didn't care.

He kissed me again, putting me at ease for a couple seconds until that intensity burned inside my body, making me want him more. I kissed him back, showing him that I wasn't scared, that I truly did mean my words, all of them. Every single one of them. I pulled that shirt of his over his head, and threw it to the ground. He kissed me over and over again, more than I thought he would. But he kept kissing me hungrily. And then started to kiss my skin, biting and nibbling at my neck. I tensed a bit, liking how he felt, liking how he kissed me, liking how he handled me and how he treated me. I wanted him.

His hand moved further down and I moved my hips up to him. If he touches me there, it will only make me want him more.

"Eli..." I moaned quietly as I pulled him closer to me. He continued to kiss my neck passionately, probably leaving marks on my body, as his hands began to fondle me lightly. My body tensed and trembled under his as he made me moan more for him.

I wanted him. And he wanted me too.

I couldn't be anymore excited or enthralled with this. The longer we kept this going, the longer I wanted to stay with him. And it would be a while.

I haven't felt anything so strong, or passionate in my life. Nothing could compare to this feeling. His skin on mine, his hands on my body, the way he made me the way I was, the way I wanted him, all of it. Feeling all of it just made me more vulnerable.

Eli had made passionate love to me.

I haven't been consumed in this much emotion before, but I wanted to drown in it. Eli made me want to just be in all of it, and I clutched on to that. As he did what he did to me, I enjoyed every second of it, hoping that it would drag on for forever.

I wanted to stay with Eli longer, to hold him more, to keep him near me. I just wanted to be with him more than anything else right now.

I couldn't help but stare into his eyes for a long while. He was watching me too, and he has been since all this happened. My face was still red but I didn't think of it as embarrassing, Eli is always just looking anyway. But he has another face to add to his collection. Hopefully, he forgets my erotic faces and pretends they never existed. But I bet he was collecting it all in his head. I know that much.

"You stare at me too much." I said quietly as I finally looked away, looking down at the sheets instead.

"I like your face." he said as he moved my hair back away from my eyes. He was still going to keep watching me this way.

"You always say that." I laughed lightly as my fingers twisted more in the sheets. I was warm here, and I never wanted to leave no matter what.

"Because I mean it."

"You're going to make me blush." I said seriously.

"That's the point, Jamie." he said as he pulled the sheets off him. "Its late, I should walk you home." he said as he picked up his pants to put on.

I noticed his back, and all those muscles he claims to not have. Then I saw the red paint stains on his body, where my hands were on him. And there was paint in his messy black hair. That was my fault too and I didn't regret it. I turned over in his bed, reaching for my pants on the floor first.

As much as I didn't want to go, I know my parents are probably freaking out over the fact that I am nowhere to be seen. I don't think I would be able to just tell them this happened, they would yell at me and tell me I have problems even though I don't.

I just like someone a lot, that's all.

I got dressed and we were going to leave but we got side tracked a bit, just staying against the wall and kissing lightly. I really had to get home but I don't want to miss something like this. I like Eli, so I don't mind spending another couple hours with him. I like it a lot. He was okay with it as just as I was, but we had to be responsible and go anyway.

It was already dark outside, no clouds in the sky, just darkness and stars. We walked slowly together, holding hands, and he told me about wanting to draw stars in the sky. How the yellow balls of light went well with the contrast of the black sky. He made me want to draw it too, it might be the only think of doing. The moon was a perfect crescent shape that reflected light from the sun. He told me how he would shade and color it and I told him that would be amazing.

"You have red paint all over in your hair." he said quietly as we walked up to my door. The lights were on which made me slightly fearful.

"I know and I like it." I said.

"It suits you." he said and smiled. Of course it does. I smiled up at him and remembered before without hesitation. It made me blush and look away because I was somewhat a little embarrassed. And he noticed too, I could tell by the way he laughed lightly. "I'll see you tomorrow, Jamie." he said.

He always says that when he walks me home. And this time he kissed my reddened cheek, making me feel hotter. I stared at him for a moment and tried to find words to reply to him with. I do that a lot apparently.

"Bye Eli." I said quietly, hoping he heard me. Hopefully, it wasn't too late. But I watched him go as my hand went to the door, searching for the knob mindlessly.

My mind was on Eli.

I know I have to put that on pause for a while because I have to face my angry parents. It is going to be a terrible thing when they start yelling at me for absolutely no reason at all. I can already feel their voices in my head. But I wish it weren't like that. I heard them quiet down as I closed the door behind me. And then I heard them getting up and walking over to see me.

"Where were you?" Mom asked quickly.

"I was with Eli." I said.

"We were worried sick for you." she said before dad could say anything about it. Mom was more furious than dad was but they're both mad anyway.

"I was working on a project with him and lost track of time." I lied smoothly, hoping it worked. Through his glasses, I could see that dad narrowed his eyes in suspicion. He can't know I'm lying.

"Is that why you have red paint in your hair and your skin, Jamie?" Mom asked. I had paint in a lot of places all over my body. All over.

"Yes." I answered. I was just standing there, defending myself because I know I can't do anything else.

"This friend of yours takes up a lot of your time." Dad said.

"We're partners." I said.

"Of course you are." Mom said quickly. "Just go wash that out of your hair." she said. I was quick to leave and go upstairs.

I probably wasn't going to wash the red paint out of my hair for a while. I wanted to remember it even though I don't need the paint to remember something as eventful as that.

I couldn't stop thinking about it, and I was happy about it too. The red paint marks can only make my memories more intense.

GREEN

Green- restful and soothing, tranquility and good luck, cheerful and relaxing.

I walked into art class with the rest of the others who were shuffling in as the bell rang. No one took my seat next to Eli, but no one would. Everyone knows he isn't one to talk or to become friends with, that's until you bump into him and apologize for it. He isn't intimidating, but he makes it clear that it might be difficult to get to him.

Just ask first.

I sat down next to Eli. I noticed he was just doodling something, even though when he doodles, he's creating a master piece anyway. He knows that. I stared at the eyes he was shading in with a black color pencil. They looked like they had color to them even though its just black and white. For him to be able to do that is amazing. I stared and stared and he didn't even seem to notice me that quickly. But I like watching him draw.

He had completely ignored Mr. Phillips for the first five minutes of class and I understood why. But soon he stopped and looked up.

"Looks like you were busy." I whispered quietly to him.

"I was." he said just as quiet. I took his sketch book from his lap and looked at the eyes. There were small freckles close to them, and by the small bridge, I bet he would have drawn a nose too. Let me guess, these are my eyes.

I wonder if I'm his muse.

He put more feeling into a plain sketch of my eyes than any picture could capture. I hated how he could do this, but I loved his skill at the same time. It made me envious. The way my eyes shined mesmerized me. The way Eli draws me always makes me go into shock, no matter what face it is. I held in a sigh. I want to be like him sometimes.

I flipped the page back to see what he did before, but it just made me even more shocked than I could have been in the first place. My heart had skipped a couple beats and my cheeks were getting hot, I could even feel it around my neck too.

To recreate one of these faces made me embarrassed. I didn't think I would know what I looked like but Eli had absolutely no problem drawing this.

If last night didn't happen, this wouldn't be here.

This sketch -not just a sketch, it was something more than that, he put more effort, more emotion, just more- this sketch was of last night I'm guessing. My hair was damp with sweat, mashing around my face lightly and on the pillow. My eyes were closed, not tightly, but anyone would be able to tell that I was tense; he drew my lashes thicker than I thought they were, and by the shading, I knew my face was red, just like right now. And my mouth, I could tell what exact moment, the exact moan, the exact feeling, just by looking at my mouth. For some reason, I just looked innocent in this, and to be honest, I was. But Eli brought this side of me out quicker than he should have. Why would he draw something so erotic of me? Does he have more? They're probably in his head.

I let go of the first page and looked at Eli. He wasn't paying attention, he barely even realized that I saw what was in his sketchbook. I put my head down on the desk because I was frustrated. I was really frustrated right now. Eli just had to draw something like that and it made me really upset, but shocked. I'm not mad he drew it, I'm mad that he's capable of capturing something like that. Its unfair.

Looking at that could be like looking in a mirror. I see what he sees when he draws me, and I can tell him right now that I sometimes don't see what he does. This whole erotic piece is not something I see but he obviously did. I should have known why he was looking at me like that. His gaze was strong, something I could barely handle.

Thinking about this right now is not a good idea.

Why would he do something like this to me?

I picked my head up and looked at Eli again, and this time, he was looking at me plainly, as if he didn't know what was going on or if he should be concerned by it in someway.

"How can you draw this?" I whispered quietly as I moved the page on the sketch book to show him the embarrassment.

"Same way you can make that face." he answered, shrugging then turning his attention back to Mr. Phillips who in fact did not care if anyone was paying attention to him or not.

"That's not funny, you can't just do this to me, Eli. I don't look like this." I said in attempt to even make it true to myself but that won't work because I know that's what I looked like, at least in Eli's eyes. He looked at me again, and was serious, his eyes scanning my face.

"I can do a better one." he said. That's not what I meant! He started to smile when my face changed. He was only messing around but I knew he really would draw another one if he wanted. He might even have more.

"Eli-"

"I won't again." he said as he took his book from me; I bet he thinks I might burn this sketch but I can't do that. I think its too amazing. But I won't be able to look at myself the same way because of that. He should know what he's doing to me.

For the rest of class, he made fun of me because I was so embarrassed by what he was thinking about me. I know what he thinks now, he can't fool me. I can show him what this feels like in my view, and I'm sure he would either hate it, or not care at all. Either way, he'd know.

After school, we walked to his place, and I was eager to see what kind of mess we made since I wasn't paying attention a lot last night. There must be red paint everywhere. I wonder what Eli will do today, what sort of master piece he will create or make me sit through. I was curious to know about his project too because he said he started it, but I bet he won't show me until its done. I just walked around inside, noting the red paint, slightly looking for where he might have his project hidden but he doesn't have to show me if he doesn't want to yet.

"So where's your project?" I asked anyway because I thought it might give me a slight advantage in knowing.

"Its somewhere around here." he said as if he lost it but he wants me to believe that. I heard something being poured down the drain but its not something that I'm not used to.

Eli is getting a bit better at all this, just a little.

He's dumping the alcohol out.

I'm hoping he doesn't lapse but I don't know when that might happen. He hasn't had any problems for a while, and that's really good. Before I was just concerned, but I don't need to be now.

"Come on Eli," I urged.

"I don't know." he said. I knew he would do that. I don't think I could just not find it but I won't look. I just went over to Eli and stood next to him, watching him dump all the alcohol from the bottles.

"Do you have another stash?" I asked.

"Not that I remember."

"Should I look?" I asked.

"Do you want to?" he looked down at me, only curious to know if he should let me. I won't look. I just want to know from him. "I don't think I have more." he said.

"Its a good thing you aren't drinking." I said and meant it.

"I know." he said plainly.

He should feel better, but its hard to know how Eli feels sometimes. For someone who can get the most emotion shown through art, he barely experiences any. It just depends on the whole thing. I left his side and went to stand by the wall. I wanted to paint the wall, maybe green. A dark emerald green would look nice. I got down on the floor and pulled out all the paint colors. I took all the greens and blues and started to mix them in a small container.

Its like a sea green but almost as dark as emerald. Its close enough. I mixed it, and mixed it, until I liked it. Its nice color. I stared at it for a while and thought to myself. I could paint a lot of things with this color. I scooted closer to the wall after a while as I dipped the small brush into the paint. I had nothing in mind that I wanted to paint but I knew I just wanted to paint. So I became absent minded.

I moved the brush on the wall, curling and drawing small swirls that branched out. I'm sure this could be a cool tattoo. I continued to branch it as far as I could reach, giving it direction and flow on the wall as if it were my own canvas. I wanted to take over all this small space with this blue emerald green.

"That's a nice color." Eli said behind me as he sat down next to me. He had gotten a brush with the same color paint. Instead of putting it on the wall though, he paints my palm instead. I looked down to see what he was doing, but I saw he was mimicking me.

"You're going to paint my body, Eli?" I asked.

"That's a good idea." he said as he tried to smile, almost getting there. I looked down and watched him paint to my wrist and up my arm lightly. It tickled me, making goosebumps form on my skin. "Its a nice color on you. Just like red." he said.

I began blushing.

And then I realized he only said that so he could see the red show up on my face. He always does. I painted the wall, making small patterns as he drew on me as well. The feeling of the brush on my skin made me feel lighter than usual, I knew I liked the feeling a lot.

He had made it up to my arm, and I thought he would stop there, he should have but I wanted him to keep going because I liked how it looked on me, it should be everywhere on me. That's what I wanted. I ended up taking off my shirt carefully so I wouldn't mess anything up. Eli drew up my shoulder and to my back, making it tickle in my skin. I knew every stroke of his hand with the brush. And soon I felt like I could literally be one with his drawings, as if I was actually one of them.

I was now his canvas.

I stopped moving only to hear his breathing behind me. Eli was silent as he painted softly on my skin. I felt him trace a line of paint on the middle of my back, as if to follow my spine. And then he branched out, making curls and swirls that I could feel. I stared at my arm as I got lost in the feeling of being painted on. The green and blue had mixed in completely and made the color entrancing. I wanted to keep this on me. I wanted Eli to draw all over me.

But when he stopped, I knew that was his limit.

I was satisfied, I wanted to keep this on me because I liked the color since it looked nice on my skin.

"You're amazing." I said to him quietly as I turned to face him. He put the brush down and looked at me with his blue eyes. He even looked like he enjoyed it but he was serious. This was all serious.

His hand moved to my face without a word, and then he started to pull me closer to him. Before I knew it, he was kissing me. I can't be shocked anymore, Eli is the only who has touched me the way he has, and I liked it. He kissed me and I let him do it. I couldn't mess up this paint, but I desperately wanted to wrap my arms around his neck so I could keep him closer to me. This was enough though.

His hands on my cheek, his lips on mine, his breath with mine, I can have all of him if I wanted to and I know he felt the same way. But as much as I want to, I know I can't. Not right now at least.

His soft lips pulled away from mine after a couple seconds of kissing me. He still stayed close to me anyway; I kept my eyes closed as I felt his soft breath on my skin, breathing lightly as he moved his hands from my face. He was that close to me, yet he wouldn't do anything else to me. I almost sighed but held it in as I moved a bit closer, pressing my forehead to his.

We sat in silence for a little while, not doing anything. Sometimes, Eli tells me how the silence is good for him, but other times, it makes him crack. Maybe since I'm here, everything might be okay for him. Of course, we just stayed like this for a long while, and didn't talk. But we understood our silence, it was different. Being silent is just the same as doing anything else together. I felt the overwhelming emotion inside my body but at the same time, I was calm, like nothing bothered.

Being with Eli can do that to me sometimes.

"I should take you home." he said after a while. It wasn't so dark outside, but I know my parents will be over joyed to know that I'm home early.

"I could stay." I said quietly.

"I want you to," he said, just as quiet.

But we both knew I had to go home. Maybe he can sneak in later and we can draw together.

Eli got up and held his hand out for me to take. I did take it, and he helped me up, not letting go. I stared up at him and wondered about a lot of things. After a couple seconds, I bent down to get my shirt off the floor and put it on. I didn't forget about the paint on my body, but I know it will be sort of hard to disguise this from my parents if they're home. I don't feel like washing this off me just yet.

Eli walked me home like he said he would of course. No second later did my parents start yelling at me when I walked into the house. I was told to wash the paint off and now I have no choice but to. I was going to do what I was told, but I wanted to think of Eli just a bit more. I wanted to see this wonderful art work he put on my body.

I looked in my mirror, twisting the upper half of my body to see a portion of my back in the reflection. I was amazed to see what Eli has done to me. It was beautiful. I wanted to think of this for a while, and of course see it again, the only way to do that though is if I draw it myself. I might have to.

A dark blue emerald green, a color I want to recreate again so I don't forget this.

PURPLE

Purple- royalty and wealth, wisdom and spiritual, exotic and artificial.

I drew part of my project on a piece of white paper as my parents talked about some psychological studies that are going on at the hospital. I was interested like usual, but I wanted to keep my focus on just how colors make and enhance people's abilities, behavior, and emotions. I think its cool that there is some kind of affect with colors.

"Jamie?" Mom sat down in front of me. I didn't realize that she stopped talking first of all. I looked up at her, then at dad. Why do they look concerned? What happened?

"What sort of issue does that friend of yours have?" Dad asked.

I knew it.

I just stared at them quietly because I know they will try to analyze every single aspect of Eli as if he is some test subject. He isn't though, I know that.

"None." I answered finally.

"Are you sure because we think-"

"Not everyone has a problem." I said to them as I continued shading in the shadows for the collage. I was drawing my back with the colored paint that Eli had drawn on me a couple days ago.

"You are changing towards people too, Jamie." Mom said.

"You've opened up more, and you show more with your expressions." Dad said. I looked at them both. I want to say that's a good thing, because it is. I should be proud that I'm getting better at that. Eli said that's the only way for art to work.

But he contradicts that the most, or so he lets me believe.

I watched my parents, they wanted to explain more but they wouldn't and I wanted to know why at least.

"He must be a good friend to you." Dad said to me but he was hinting something else. But he wasn't catching on. Friend is an understatement, and I hope it stays that way.

"He's a good person," I said.

"You sure he has no issues?" Mom asked.

"Mom!"

"I was just wondering." she said and that made me sort of upset. There is nothing wrong with Eli.

"He is fine. You don't need to break down every part of his mind to know if he has psychological issues." I said as I got up, taking my pencils and papers. Its about time I go to my room because I have been down here for too long.

I walked upstairs to my room, and turned on the lights to put my stuff down. It was already nine p.m. and its Friday night. I don't do much on weekends anymore. This project is due anytime soon, which is like next week, and I really need to get all these sketches together. I have a good number but its not half of what I want yet.

I'm putting everything I've drawn together in one place. I have a bunch of things of Eli too, and I don't mind that. I love everything I draw of him. I even have the things he drew of me, and I know I will keep that too. Its a nice addition to my project. Everything I have is something I cherish. I haven't drawn this much before I met Eli, now its just taken over my life.

I took out all my papers that I had started gluing together on a bigger white cardboard. This whole thing was coming out nicely, well I thought it was.

I heard my window moving, but I didn't mind it because it was Eli. He said he would show up tonight, so I basically waited. I was just mad that he gets to see my project and I don't even have the slightest clue what his is. He did say that he was doing the same thing I was but its probably going to be so much better. Its going to put mine to shame.

"This is not fair, Eli. You can't just see my project when you don't let me see yours." I said quickly, trying to cover it up. But he walked over to me, laughing lightly.

"I'll let you see it sometime, maybe tomorrow." he said and sat down. He had put his hands on all my sketches and pulled them out from under my bed. How unfair. He was still smiling as he went through it, looking at all the things I've drawn in the past couple weeks.

"Can you not look at these?" I asked.

"I want to." he said as he pulled some of them up. He always tells me that his favorite one is the sketch of his back but I will never understand why. He looked at some more, and found some random stuff, then some of his face. All his smiles, his happy eyes, his better days. "You've finally got there." he said quietly.

I didn't know what he meant, but I didn't ask.

"So, what kinds of things do you have drawn for your project, unless you're doing the exact same thing I am." I said.

"Well its not exactly the same." he said.

"You mean its better?" I asked.

"Not really." he answered plainly. I wish he wouldn't lie to me. I looked down, almost beginning to laugh because he said that. He just doesn't understand. "You can see what I have done. Which is the whole thing." he said.

"Stop bragging, Eli." I said quickly.

"I'm not the bragging type." he said and put all my papers together. Right. But Eli does it discretely, he doesn't have to say anything to brag. He knows he's the best here, we all know that. I took my papers from his hand and moved them somewhere else as I pushed the board under my bed.

"What kind of sketches do you have on yours?" I asked.

"Just the things I like." he answered. When I looked at him, I saw him smiling. More and more everyday, he smiles. I like how he does that, its nice. I was beginning to smile with him.

"Is it colorful?" I asked.

"It is." he said. "It has all the colors I could think of." he said. I wanted to see it, that's what I was aiming for. I just wanted to see it and look at it. "I'll show you tomorrow." he said as he got up.

"Don't tell me you're leaving." I complained.

"I don't want to take away from your night." he said and I got up with him. I stood in front of him, and smoothed out the ruffles from his black jacket. It matched his sleek black curly hair, strands passing over his blue eyes.

Why does Eli take consider me so much?

"Don't say goodnight just yet." I said quietly as I moved my hand to his. He pursed his lips tightly, still watching me with his blue eyes that I liked so much, that I wanted to color so much. His other hand touched my cheek lightly as he moved closer to me. At least he isn't leaving yet.

He kissed me softly, just like he always does. I moved my arm around his neck lightly, hoping that would make him stay. He didn't show any signs of letting go of me and that made it better. He kissed me more as his fingers caressed my face, moving lightly to my hair as I pulled him closer to me. The more he kissed me, the more I wanted him to stay.

My arms tightened around him, not giving him the will to let me go. But he kissed me rougher, and I kissed him just as roughly. We began to get greedy. Everything I thought about was wiped out of my mind because kissing him was the only thing that had my attention. We were moving back, just aimlessly moving until I felt the bed hit the back of my knees.

He didn't wait a second to get me on that bed. I took this as an opportunity to have him all to myself. Eli got on top of me, his hand twisting in my hair as he continued to kiss me. I enjoyed having his mouth on mine, kissing me this way. I enjoyed him holding me like this, and touching me like this. I kept him closer, feeling his body on mine. It reminded me of before, making me want to do it again.

My urges got so strong, but I could feel his too. He wanted this.

Well that's what I thought before he pulled away from me, far enough to actually stop this.

He breathed on me for a second, then he kissed me again and again; he kissed my lips, my cheek, my jawline, all the way down my neck too. I bit my lip to keep in any sounds. But I whimpered silently when he kissed my neck more, his hand going in my shirt. I wanted him to go further, to continue this.

But then he really stopped, getting off me and off my bed.

"Goodnight, Jamie." he said as we talked to my window.

"Eli, that's not fair." I complained as I sat up. He turned and smiled at me as he opened my window. I didn't think he would do something like that to me, but he did. I ran my hand through my hair as I watched him go, still smiling. That was the last face I saw of him as he let himself out.

I fell back on my bed and sighed. That was not fair.

I stared up at my ceiling and thought about what he was doing to me. How I liked it, how I wanted more of him, and how I wish he wouldn't do something like that to me. I sat up again and looked around my room. After a while of staring, I got out of bed and took what I was working on earlier so I could go downstairs again.

My parents were still talking about psychological things that was way beyond my own comprehension of life. I sat down quietly on the couch as they talked about things, mentioning me in that process sometimes, telling each other what direction I should be going in, what's best for me, what my future should be.

I don't know what my future might be because at this point I don't care much. I know what I want to study and I know I like art. If anything, I know only those two factors will direct me. I colored in the shadows, thinking what if I were to color this with the actual blue emerald green. It would be nice to remember that. Maybe Eli can paint me again, maybe even more than just one more time hopefully.

"Jamie? Can you come down- Oh, you're already here." Mom had stumbled in when she saw me sitting on the couch and dad was right behind her. I looked at her plainly as she stared down at me. What is she concerned about this time? I know there isn't anything wrong with me.

"We wanted to ask you something." Dad said.

"I hope its not about the people I hang out with or what emotional problems I'm experiencing because that isn't something I really want to talk about." I said quietly as I looked at my work again. They're going to talk about people's issues like usual.

"No, its not that. Well, we wanted to talk about your behavior." Mom said. I narrowed my eyes but I still looked at my paper. "We noticed the good change in you, the very good change. And we were hoping that it wouldn't affect what your future should be." she said.

"If its a good change, you shouldn't worry." I said.

"Jamie, we are concerned." She said, trying to get me to listen to her. I stared at her finally, wondering what she could possibly be concerned about. I didn't do anything, at least, I hope I didn't because that would be terrible.

"Why are you always so happy all the time? Or why are you always so absorbed in drawing? You said that was temporary." Dad said.

"I'm sorry."

"Don't start apologizing, Jamie." Mom said quickly.

"I'm just having fun, I guess. Its nice." I shrugged as I looked up at them. Mom's anger fled from her as she looked at dad; they haven't heard something like that. I'm a quiet kid, I don't do much, so I guess this is a shocker to them. I can understand.

"Its him, isn't it?" Dad asked.

"Eli is not my only friend."

"But he's the one you spend the most time with, the one you talk about the most, the one that we only see you with." Dad said.

Why are they doing this to me?

"He's my friend." I said as I tried to make it believable. I held on to my pencil tightly as they still watched me.

I'm not going to help my feelings for Eli, and even if I could, I would make sure that I would like him the same way I do now. I would never change something like that, it would be unfair to me and him. I like him and that's it. But I'm not going to tell mom and dad that because it would lead to my doom of course. They will judge me out loud and make things terrible when its not a big deal of course.

"Jamie-"

"I should be getting to bed. Its late." I said as I got up, getting my stuff. If they're going to analyze me, then lets give them another symptom of my problem; getting up and storming out. I don't want to be badgered the way they do to me, for once, I just want them to be okay with it. My future isn't in danger or something like that, I have everything under control so they don't need to worry about me once bit.

All I know is that I am not going to give up on Eli if they think its beneficial which it isn't. I like him, and I like what we do and its fine.

YELLOW

Yellow- cheery and warm, frustration and anger, overwhelming and sadness.

Eli had found a way to stall me from seeing his glorious project and it made me mad because I was so excited to see it. I would love to see his master piece but he says it doesn't feel like the right time to do that. Its unfair but I had to be patient because he said so.

"Okay, how about tonight?" I asked, still attempting to see because I think it will be worth the sight. He knows that. He stopped writing and looked at me. "I'm not doing anything after school." I said.

"Why does this mean so much to you?" he asked me.

"I'm really curious to see because you drop hints, Eli. Don't pretend that you don't. You're basically telling me that it will put what i have to shame." I said quickly as I put my bag on the table. School is almost over and I could feel my excitement bubbling, over flowing throughout my body.

"Its not that great." he shrugged.

"You are lying." I said quickly. He began laughing as he put his eyes back on his paper again. I thought he would at least say yes but he won't. He just smiled and laughed like he has been for a while, I even wanted to start laughing but I held it in.

"Okay, I'll show you later." he said.

"Alright, that's better." I said and sat back in my seat. With only a few minutes left, I knew I didn't have to wait long. But I know Eli will stall, I know him well enough for that.

"I still don't see why you care." Eli said.

"I like what you can do. I think its amazing." I said as I looked into his blue eyes. He was serious, and I wondered why he wouldn't smile, then again, its always a rare thing that I can't force. I wasn't surprised. I stared back at him, wondering if he was going to say something to that.

The bell rang and everyone got up, taking their stuff and shuffling out into the hallway as the bell still rang. I sat there with Eli for a second, still waiting on him as he put his stuff away. I got up and put my bag over my shoulder.

"So we can just go over to-"

"How about we go to your place for a while?" Eli cut in as he took his bag. I looked at him, slightly shocked that he would say that after he promised me something. But then I knew he was stalling again, of course he would do something like that. I looked down, pushing my hair back after I knew.

"Eli." I complained.

"I promised I'd show you." he said. "But you have to give me an hour or so." he said as if it was nothing. Alright, I can do that much I guess. He wants another hour to finish up or make it special, then fine, but I just want to know what it is and how beautiful it is.

"Fine, then we can go to my house now, then you can leave and get your hour, then I'm coming to see that project, Eli. I mean it." I said and hoped he knew just that. I will not let him get away with not showing me because this project is due Friday and its Tuesday right now.

"I know, trust me." he said as he walked ahead of me. I sighed and followed behind him mindlessly. I always follow behind him. Eli is the one I follow, the one I look up to, the one I like. I wasn't surprised that I was so attached to him now, its obvious that I would be.

I like Eli and everything he is.

I noticed that he was a bit quieter on the walk home. The way he talked changed, that's if he said anything at all. I know what's going on, he's about to cave in again, but I know he has the strength to handle it anyway. I don't doubt him. But the way he talked reminded me of so much, I have to make sure that he isn't distracted by anything that could set him off. I thought being outside might make him happy or something. The sky is clear, there are no clouds and the sun is shining brightly but somehow, Eli was a bit quieter.

"Are you okay, Eli?" I asked him when we got to my house.

"Yeah, I guess I'm a bit tired." he said as he put his bag down. "I've been working a lot, so I guess it caught up to me." he said as he rubbed the back of his neck.

"Well I think there's food here, I'm hoping at least." I said, and started laughing. He said that the first time I came to his place, and I still remember that day and the days after that. "You should probably be getting more sleep." I said.

"I know." he said and he truly does know that for sure, he always knows. But it happens, he gets drunk and he just sits there, pondering about things that he would never tell me about, things that I would never be able to talk about with him because he won't let me know.

He just says that there are things that he can't control, that he wants to take out of him, that he wants to get rid of. I want to help him, but I don't get further than what he lets me know. And I would never break him apart just to know what he's thinking, I would never on my life.

"Tell me you won't let anything happen." I said as I went back over to him. Moving the wrinkles of his shirt like I always do. I was touching his shirt but in my mind, I was getting a feel for his body; sometimes, that's my excuse. He was almost smiling, he was almost there. He took my hand lightly, and held it.

"I won't. I'll be fine." he promised me. Its a good thing that he's holding on at least.

For the day, we sat and doodled things while we talked about things. And possibly cuddled and kissed, but that wasn't too much. Then my parents got home and I couldn't house Eli because my parents are mad enough at everything and me that I said what I said. I can't win with them, so I don't want to get in trouble or make Eli unstable. Eli said I could come over later if I wanted to, and I just might too, but I need to solve all this with my parents.

"Why are you antsy?" Mom asked.

"I-I-"

"Something you're hiding?" she asked as she walked closer to me. I don't hide things, I don't ever hide things. But she was about to corner me on this subject and I can't get passed out that easily.

"No, mom, I don't have anything to hide from you." I said quickly as I grabbed my bag. I should go upstairs right now and not come back here until Eli calls me.

"Jamie-"

"I have homework to work on, I'll be in my room for a while."

"Do not go anywhere, Jamie." Mom got in before I could turn my back. I tried but I couldn't disobey her. There was no way I would get away with something like that and I knew that of course, but she still had to test her authority as if I would challenge her. I faced her and dad and waited for them to say something.

"You are too consumed with that friend of yours." Dad said.

"You know people cannot live without human contact, whether if its their mother or father, or anyone. You know Eli lost his parents, and he had no one. I just wanted to be his friend because can't go on by himself." I explained myself quickly.

"You are not just friends, Jamie." Mom said just as fast; I could hear her rage and anger as she said that, but what stuck out the most was her shock. "We know, Jamie."

"Okay, so you know. What about it? What's wrong? Are you going to say that there is something wrong with me, that I have a problem?" I asked. "I always have to suppress everything because you like to analyze people like they're subjects when they aren't. We are all just humans." I said.

I want to believe they're just looking out for me, they are my parents, that's what they do. But this is too much, this is all too much. They can't just do this.

"We all feel the same thing." Mom said.

"You even have to know that's a false statement mom, no one feels the exact same way for anything or anyone. That's what makes us different. You told me this." I said to her. I could tell that I was making her more upset than she should be, but she knows what she's doing and its unfair.

"Why are you mad?" Dad asked. I turned to him, ready to answer, but I didn't. I couldn't say what I wanted to. It will be impossible to get past something like that. So I pursed my lips in a hard line and looked at the ground, keeping quiet.

"You're being defensive." Mom said.

"I have to go do homework." I said and made my run for it to go upstairs. I would have to stay here until Eli calls me to come over. But I don't want to stay here for a while.

I pulled out all my color pencils and some paper. This is the one way I know how to take my rage out. I picked all the reds from the box, and the yellows and orange. A fire, a big fire, one so big that it can swallow me whole without hesitation.

I want to think that I was being defensive, I probably was, but I don't want my parents doing this to me. I don't want them saying that I have problems, that there's something wrong with me. I know I'm fine, everything about me is fine. I believe that. Mom and Dad don't have to worry, its nothing. Its just nothing. I can't have anything good in my life without them saying it.

I got down everything I could until I couldn't feel my hands, until I had no more rage to get down on paper. Then it got dark and I had to stop, I just had to. There was nothing left. I push the rage filled paper to the floor and ran my hands through my hair as I tried to calm down, only wanting to. I can't get out of control because that would make everything worse. I don't deserve that, I need to be calm.

My phone vibrated on my pillow. I reached for it, already knowing it was Eli texting me. I guess he's ready, and I know I am too. This will probably be one of the good things that has happened today, the one good thing. Eli knows how to make me smile, at least I have him to lean on. I got up and took my jacket, ready to go. I had to get past my parents somehow but I can just tell them that I'm leaving. They shouldn't care that I'm going out to see Eli. They shouldn't mind it.

I walked down stairs and looked around. Silence was the only thing I heard. I know my parents aren't early sleepers for sure, they never were. They might be talking silently about me and what's going wrong with me. Which is nothing. I just fixed my collar as I headed outside as I quietly could. I need to run over there without getting stopped in the midst of it. I won't even be gone long so it should be fine too.

I walked quietly, my hands in my pockets as I looked up at the dark sky. The stars were out but to me, it seemed only boring. There was nothing extra ordinary about the sky tonight, it was just the same. I sighed and looked forward, trying to take in the clear air as I thought peacefully. Maybe this walk was something I needed.

I noticed a woman leaning over someone frantically. There was a car behind her, the headlights on. She was calling for help and at the same time, fumbling with her phone. I know I can't do much, but I wanted to help as best as I could. Eli won't mind if I show up a little late, but this was happening out front of his apartment building anyway. I walked over to the lady who was calling for the paramedics, crying and saying how scared she was of this.

But I only stared at the person who was on the floor.

I felt my heart tug in my chest as I covered my mouth. I had mentally paused as I looked down at Eli's body on the ground, bleeding out as he laid there unconscious. I fell to the ground, grasping on to him as I felt his body. He was going cold already. And I started to panic as I shook him, hoping he would wake up.

"Eli, wake up." I shook him, and I kept doing it, but every second ended up being a second that he didn't respond. "Eli please...don't do this." I started to cry as I tried to wake him. I tried so hard. But he wouldn't move, he just wouldn't.

And this woman was telling me how sorry she was, how she didn't see him, how she couldn't stop. But I didn't care about her, how can I blame her? What's the point of doing something like that? I just wanted Eli to be better, I was hoping that he would be fine.

The paramedics came and I didn't here anything about him being dead or something like that, but I heard that they found that he was intoxicated. It made me cry harder to know that, to know that he promised me that he wouldn't cave. I know that him getting hit wasn't his fault but he shouldn't have been drunk. Maybe he would have noticed that lady coming and he wouldn't have been hit. I wanted him to not be hit.

Today has been the worst day. I didn't expect this to happen. I was frustrated and angry and upset and I was raging and crying. This should not happen, this should not be happening to me or him. Eli should be okay, that's what I need to tell myself. He will be okay.

BLACK

Black- death and mournful, menacing and evil, unhappiness and depression. Lack of all sensation.

I paced around in the hospital waiting room, wondering what was taking that doctor so long. I know I just got here, but I needed to know if Eli was okay. He didn't deserve this, he never deserved this, not with everything he went through. I ran my hand through my hair repetitively, panicking out loud and inside my head. This is not happening.

My face had been dried with tears, my eyes were puffy and blurry, and I can't feel my insides. I was numb but at the same time, I was over flowing with all kinds of emotions. I didn't know what to feel or how to handle it. I made sure to think positive. I had to.

When I saw the doctor, I ran up to her almost about to start crying. She looked plain and bare as if she felt nothing. I wanted to believe there was something, anything.

"Is he okay?" I asked. She had looked away for a second, and when she didn't answer me fast enough, I felt the tears weld up in my eyes again. "Is Eli okay?" I asked again, feeling my throat close up, tighter and tighter every second. I could barely even breathe.

"I am so sorry." she said quietly.

She's sorry.

"There was nothing else we could do."

I was staring right through her, watching everything fade before my eyes. Eli's gone, he's gone. Just like that, he's gone. But earlier we were just together. He told me he was going to show me his project that was so amazing. We were talking earlier, he was holding me earlier. Everything was fine earlier, I don't know how this happened.

If only I had stayed with him, if only I hadn't let him go, if only I had snuck him up to my room, if only I had left earlier.

If only!

I turned away, going numb as I stared aimlessly at the wall. What am I going to do now, what's going to happen now, how am I going to go on now. I lost a great person in my life, I lost someone I cared about, someone I loved, someone I needed. I don't understand. I felt the tears but I wasn't processing this. I don't understand any of this.

"Jamie?" That sounded like my mom. I turned around and saw both my parents standing there, looking at me. I called them and told them what happened, and they didn't hesitate to come to get me. I stared at them and realized they're the only ones I could go to because Eli isn't here.

He's gone.

I ran to them, and started crying harder. Mom was already prepared for me to become hysteric, who wouldn't turn out this way, I just lost someone I loved. Mom hugged me tightly and I cried hard into her shoulder. For once they aren't doing anything to mess this up, to make it worse. But I didn't care. I just cried and cried, shaking and trembling as I cried worse than I ever could.

"He's dead. He's dead." I cried into her shoulder. Her fingers ran through my hair as she shushed me, trying to calm me down.

"Its going to be okay." She said quietly as she continued to pet my hair. I didn't believe her, I couldn't even though I tried. All this happened too fast, I didn't see it coming.

I felt like I was going to fall, like I was going to be swallowed up in my guilt and anger and sorrow. I couldn't hold myself up anymore. It hurt so much that I couldn't breathe either, I was clutching my stomach and trying to breathe but it didn't work. I was slowly dying on the inside, and I was being sucked down into a spiraling world. I still cried, telling myself that I'm delusional and everything will be okay. But he's dead and I can't be in denial.

"Jamie, its going to be fine." Mom tried to get a hold of me but I was blacking out from the pain in my chest, the pain of my heart trying to swallow itself.

It won't be fine, it won't ever be fine.

Eli was probably the best person in my life and to have him gone in a way like that does not make sense to me.

Mom tried to look me in the eyes but it didn't work because I didn't want to look at her. I didn't want to look at anyone. No one. I ran my hand through my hair as I took a step back, I didn't want to be touched either. I kept grabbing for air as I felt my chest cave in.

He can't be gone.

He was just here.

"Jamie." Dad said when he caught me staring at the ground. I looked up at him but my eyes were still blurry with tears that were being forced.

They didn't say anything to me and that made it worse. I gripped my hair tightly as my mind tried to wrap around the fact that Eli is dead and will never come back. I was overwhelmed with everything and I just wanted it to stop, I just wanted it to stop now and leave me alone. I can't take it anymore. I could barely breathe or think, or feel, or anything. No one deserves, no one should have to know what this feels like.

"Jamie, its going to be fine. Just believe us." Mom said as she tried to hold me again, but I wouldn't let her. She knows what Eli meant to me, and if she didn't then she'll know soon enough.

I fell to the ground, still crying, feeling my tears get on my shirt and neck.

"Make it stop." I cried to them. "I can't take it anymore, just make the pain stop." I wanted them to help me because I felt the stinging pain, the awful pain of losing someone I cared for so much. The pain of everything that was worth it gone. I couldn't stop it on my own, I will feel terrible on my own.

Mom got down beside me and it didn't stop me from crying. There is no way to make the pain stop. We all know that, but I want it to go away, to leave me alone because it hurt. But every second I thought about Eli being with me a few hours ago and then dead now made me cry harder.

Its not fair!

I cried for hours, I could barely get a hold of myself anymore. I was in denial about being in denial; for hours I thought it was a dream, or I had some kind of chance that Eli wasn't dead. But I know he is because we would be sitting together and drawing if he were actually here. I would be in his loft, looking at his project, at the wall, at him. I would be with him. If anything could bring him back, I would sacrifice it but I can't. Apparently in the real world, there isn't a way to bring people back like that. So I have to accept it.

Eli didn't have parents with him or siblings or anyone. I was the only one he knew and had and that's okay.

On Thursday, I had a memorial service for him. I thought it would be just me and him, but I was surprised to see people from our school showing up. It was raining and dreary, yet they came anyway, and they had left flowers and nice things for him in on his grave. They told me they didn't know him well but said that he must have been cool, or nice, or fun to hang out. But everyone knew he was talented most of all. What made me slightly happy was that Eli wasn't alone in this, he had people who wanted to be his friend, and that was the one thing that made me smile about it. Eli wasn't alone. I don't even think he thought he was completely alone in this world either. There were people that cared. I cared.

After a while, I had built up the nerves to go to his loft. I wanted to keep some things before services and authorities take everything. I walked inside the quietness, I remembered how many times we were here, everything we did and how much fun we had. It was nice. I walked over to the wall and watched it. He had painted eyes in the center around all the colors of everything else he painted. They were big green eyes, with thick lashes. I'm sure he would have drawn freckles under them.

I ran my fingers over the wall, feeling the dry paint of every color. I knew each brush stroke that he used just by touching it.

If I don't leave, I'll end up staying and crying harder than I did before.

I found some papers, some drawings, then the pile of drawings of me, but it seemed like there wasn't much, and I know Eli drew more of me. Maybe they're hidden under his bed or something like that. I reached for something but then my fingers ran over something hard and smooth, it was a board. I lost my breath. His project? I pulled it out slowly, hoping that I could build up the strength to just leave but I wanted to look. I wanted to see what his final project was.

It was a collage of everything he had of me, every face I made and emotion, anything human. Some were drawn on paper, some were drawn on the board. But it was colorful with green for my eyes. I didn't breathe, I barely couldn't as I stared at what he could do. Eli was amazing. I didn't want to believe that he would turn this in but he was. I traced my fingers over his signature at the bottom, that reminded me of him so much. My vision blurred as I covered my mouth, trying to hold it in as best as I could before anything happens.

But this was amazing.

I picked up one paper that wasn't glued yet and looked at it. He draws every face I have ever made, and he gets it down right. Its almost as if looking in a mirror. I flipped the paper over because I saw some writing on the back.

I love you.

That's what it was. He loves me. He knew I loved him, he didn't have to ask me. I loved him so much.

I cried silently, covering my face so all I would see is darkness. Everything started rushing back to me and I wished that it wouldn't. I missed Eli, I missed him so much and I want him back.
All these colors, all these drawings and paintings and everything will remind me of him, everything about him and what I loved.
Eli didn't die alone, I am still here for him.